TREATS

just great recipes

GENERAL INFORMATION

The level of difficulty of the recipes in this book is expressed as a number
from 1 (simple) to 3 (difficult).

TREATS
just great recipes
risotto

MᶜRAE BOOKS

SERVES 4
PREPARATION 15 min
COOKING 40 min
DIFFICULTY level 1

Risotto
with tomato and fresh basil

Melt 2 tablespoons of the butter in a large saucepan over medium heat. Add the onion and sauté until transparent, 3–4 minutes. • Add the tomatoes and mix well. Cook until the tomatoes have broken down and the mixture is slightly thickened, about 20 minutes. • Melt 2 tablespoons of the remaining butter in a large frying pan over medium heat. Add the rice and sauté for 2 minutes. • Pour in the wine and and cook until it evaporates. • Stir in the tomato sauce and basil. • Begin adding the stock, 1/2 cup (125 ml) at a time, cooking and stirring until each addition has been absorbed and the rice is tender, 15–18 minutes. • Stir in the remaining butter and the Parmesan. Season with salt and pepper. • Remove from the heat and let rest for 1 minute. • Garnish with the extra basil and serve hot.

1/3 cup (90 g) butter
1 small onion, finely chopped
2 cups (500 g) peeled and chopped tomatoes
1³/₄ cups (350 g) risotto rice
1/3 cup (90 ml) dry white wine
3 cups (750 ml) vegetable stock (homemade or bouillon cube), boiling
20 basil leaves, torn + extra, to garnish
1/4 cup (30 g) freshly grated Parmesan
Salt and freshly ground black pepper

SERVES 4

PREPARATION 15 min

COOKING 40 min

DIFFICULTY level 2

Risotto
flambé with apple brandy

Melt half the butter in a large frying pan over medium heat. • Add the apples, pancetta, juniper berries, and bay leaf. Sauté until the pancetta is lightly browned and the apples are tender, 5–6 minutes. • Add 2 tablespoons of brandy and let it evaporate. Remove from the heat and discard the juniper berries and bay leaf. • Melt the remaining butter in a large saucepan over medium heat. Add the shallots and sauté until tender, about 3 minutes. • Add the rice and sauté for 2 minutes. • Begin adding the stock, $1/2$ cup (125 ml) at a time, cooking and stirring until each addition has been absorbed and the rice is tender, 15–18 minutes. • Season with salt and pepper. Remove from the heat and add the Parmesan. Mix well. • Preheat the broiler (grill) on a high setting. • Grease a large ovenproof dish. • Spoon a layer of the risotto into the dish. Add a layer of the apple and pancetta mixture and a layer of Gruyère. Repeat until all the ingredients are in the dish. • Broil until the top is lightly browned, about 5 minutes. • Drizzle with the remaining brandy. Light with a match and serve while the brandy is still flaming.

$1/4$ cup (60 g) butter
2 large ripe apples, cored and sliced
4 oz (125 g) pancetta, chopped
6 juniper berries, lightly crushed
1 bay leaf
Generous $1/3$ cup (100 ml) apple brandy (Calvados)
2 shallots, finely chopped
2 cups (400 g) risotto rice
4 cups (1 liter) vegetable stock, (homemade or bouillon cube), boiling
Salt and freshly ground black pepper
$1/3$ cup (50 g) freshly grated Parmesan cheese
4 oz (125 g) Gruyère or other firm, tasty cheese, thinly sliced

Risotto
with trout and ginger

Heat half the oil in a large frying pan over medium heat. • Add the trout and sauté until cooked, 3–4 minutes. Remove from the heat. • Heat the remaining oil in a the same pan over medium heat. Add the shallot and sauté until tender, about 3 minutes. • Add the rice and sauté for 2 minutes. • Add the wine and cook until it has evaporated, 2–3 minutes. • Begin adding the stock, 1/2 cup (125 ml) at a time, cooking and stirring until each addition has been absorbed and the rice is tender, 15–18 minutes. • Stir in the ginger. Season with salt and pepper. • Add the trout and its cooking juices and mix well. • Serve hot.

1/3 cup (90 ml) extra-virgin olive oil
8 oz (250 g) trout fillets, cut into small cubes
1 shallot, finely chopped
1 3/4 cups (350 g) risotto rice
1/3 cup (90 ml) dry white wine
3 cups (750 ml) vegetable stock, (homemade or bouillon cube), boiling
1 teaspoon fresh minced ginger
Salt and freshly ground black pepper

SERVES 4

PREPARATION 10 min

COOKING 1 h

DIFFICULTY level 2

Risotto

with saffron and squid

Heat 2 tablespoons of oil in a large frying pan over medium heat.
• Add 1 shallot and sauté until tender, about 3 minutes. • Add the
squid, cover, and cook over low heat until tender, 30 minutes.
Remove from the heat and drain, reserving the cooking juices.
• Heat 2 tablespoons of the oil in the same pan over medium heat.
Add the remaining shallot and sauté until tender, 3 minutes. • Add
the rice and sauté for 2 minutes. Pour in the wine and cook until
it has evaporated, 2–3 minutes. Add the saffron. • Begin adding the
stock, $\frac{1}{2}$ cup (125 ml) at a time, cooking and stirring until each
addition has been absorbed and the rice is tender, 15–18 minutes.
• Remove from the heat and add 2 tablespoons of oil. Season with
salt and pepper. • Heat the remaining oil in a small frying pan
over medium heat. Add the garlic and sauté until pale gold,
2 minutes. Add the reserved
cooking juices and season
with salt and pepper.
Cook until the sauce
is slightly thickened.
• Remove and
discard the garlic.
• Spoon the risotto on a
serving dish. Arrange the
squid on top and drizzle with the
sauce. • Serve hot.

$\frac{1}{2}$ cup (125 ml) extra virgin olive oil
2 shallots, finely chopped
1 lb (500 g) baby squid, cleaned and
    sliced
$1\frac{3}{4}$ cups (350 g) risotto rice
$\frac{1}{3}$ cup (90 ml) dry white wine
6–8 saffron strands
3 cups (750 ml) vegetable stock,
    (homemade or bouillon cube),
    boiling
Salt and freshly ground white pepper
1 clove garlic, lightly crushed but whole

9

SERVES 4
PREPARATION 15 min
COOKING 1 h
DIFFICULTY level 1

Risotto
with sausage and tuscan kale

Cook the lentils in a small pot of boiling water until tender, 30–35 minutes. Drain well. • Cook the kale in a large pot of salted boiling water until tender, 15–20 minutes. Drain well and chop coarsely. • Melt 2 tablespoons of the butter in a large saucepan over medium heat. Add the shallots and sauté until tender, about 3 minutes. Add the thyme and sausages and sauté until the sausages are browned, 2–3 minutes. • Add the rice and sauté for 2 minutes. • Pour in the cognac and cook until it evaporates. • Add the wine and cook until it evaporates. • Begin adding the stock, 1/2 cup (125 ml) at a time, cooking and stirring until each addition has been absorbed and the rice is tender, 15–18 minutes. • Remove from the heat and stir in the Parmesan and remaining butter. Cover and let rest for 2 minutes. Remove and discard the thyme. • Serve hot.

1 cup (100 g) brown lentils
8 oz (250 g) Tuscan kale
   or savoy cabbage
3 tablespoons butter
2 shallots, finely chopped
Sprig of thyme
5 oz (150 g) Italian pork sausages,
   skinned and broken into pieces
1 3/4 cups (350 g) risotto rice
1/4 cup (60 ml) cognac
1/3 cup (90 ml) dry white wine
3 cups (750 ml) vegetable stock,
   (homemade or bouillon cube),
   boiling
Salt and freshly ground black pepper
1/2 cup (60 g) freshly grated Parmesan

SERVES 4

PREPARATION 15 min

COOKING 45 min

DIFFICULTY level 2

Risotto Torte
with ham and gorgonzola

Melt 2 tablespoons of the butter in a large frying pan over medium heat. Add the onion and sauté until transparent, about 3 minutes. • Add the rice and sauté for 2 minutes. • Pour in the wine and cook until it evaporates. • Begin adding the stock, $1/2$ cup (125 ml) at a time, cooking and stirring until each addition has been absorbed and the rice is tender, 15–18 minutes. • Remove from the heat and add the Parmesan and 1 tablespoon of butter. Mix well and transfer to a bowl. Let cool. • Melt half the remaining butter in a medium frying pan over medium-high heat. Add half the risotto and level it out using the back of a spoon. Sauté until lightly browned, 2–3 minutes. • Cover with the ham and sprinkle with half the Gorgonzola. Cover with the remaining risotto and level the surface using the back of a spoon. Slide the torte onto a plate. Cover with another plate and flip. • Melt the remaining butter in the frying pan. Slip the torte back into the pan and cook until lightly browned, 3–4 minutes. • Melt the remaining Gorgonzola with the cream in a double boiler. Add the walnuts and season with salt and pepper. Serve the torte in slices drizzled with the sauce.

$1/3$ cup (90 g) butter
1 large onion, finely chopped
2 cups (400 g) risotto rice
$1/3$ cup (90 ml) dry white wine
4 cups (1 liter) beef stock, (homemade or bouillon cube), boiling
Large pinch saffron strands
$1/3$ cup (50 g) freshly grated Parmesan
4 oz (125 g) cooked ham, sliced
8 oz (250 g) Gorgonzola cheese, cut into small cubes
Generous $3/4$ cup (200 ml) heavy (double) cream
Salt and freshly ground black pepper
$1/3$ cup (30 g) chopped walnuts

Risotto
with walnuts and garbanzo beans

Heat the oil and butter in a large frying pan over medium heat. Add the onion and sauté until transparent, 3–4 minutes. • Add the rice and sauté for 2 minutes. • Pour in the wine and cook until it evaporates, 2–3 minutes. • Add ½ cup (125 ml) of the stock and cook until it is absorbed. • Add the garbanzo peas, walnuts, and tomato concentrate and mix well. Keep adding the stock, ½ cup (125 ml) at a time, cooking and stirring until each addition has been absorbed and the rice is tender, 15–18 minutes. • Remove from the heat and season with salt and pepper. Stir in the Parmesan and garnish with the sage. • Serve hot.

2 tablespoons extra-virgin olive oil
1 tablespoon butter
1 small onion, finely chopped
1¾ cups (350 g) risotto rice
⅓ cup (90 ml) dry white wine
3 cups (750 ml) vegetable stock, (homemade or bouillon cube), boiling
1 cup (250 g) canned garbanzo beans (chickpeas), drained
Scant 1 cup (90 g) coarsely chopped walnuts
1 teaspoon tomato concentrate (paste)
½ cup (60 g) freshly grated Parmesan
3 sage leaves, finely chopped, to garnish

Risotto
with spring vegetables

Remove the tough outer leaves from the artichokes. Cut off the top third of the leaves. Cut in half and scrape out any fuzzy inner core, Slice finely. Place in a bowl of water with the lemon juice. • Heat 2 tablespoons of oil in a large frying pan over medium heat. Add the garlic and sauté until pale gold, 2–3 minutes. Discard the garlic. • Add the mushrooms and sauté for 5 minutes. • Drain the artichokes and add to the pan. Sauté until tender, 10 minutes. Set aside. • Meanwhile, heat 2 tablespoons of oil in another large frying pan over medium heat. Add half the onion and sauté until transparent, 3–4 minutes. Add the zucchini, asparagus, peas, bell pepper, and tomatoes. Season with salt and pepper. Cook until tender, 6–8 minutes. Set aside. • Heat the remaining oil in a large frying pan over medium heat. Add the remaining onion and sauté until transparent, 3–4 minutes. Add the rice and sauté for 2 minutes. • Begin adding the stock, ½ cup (125 ml) at a time, cooking and stirring until each addition has been absorbed and the rice is tender, 15–18 minutes. • Stir in the vegetables, butter, and Parmesan. Garnish with the parsley and serve hot.

2 artichokes

Juice of 1 lemon

2 small tomatoes, peeled and chopped

1/3 cup (90 ml) extra-virgin olive oil

1 clove garlic, lightly crushed but whole

5 oz (150 g) button mushrooms, sliced

2 small onions, finely chopped

4 medium zucchini (courgettes), cut into small cubes

12 asparagus tips, cut into short sections

1 cup (150 g) fresh or frozen peas

1 small yellow bell pepper (capsicum), seeded and chopped

Salt and freshly ground black pepper

1¾ cups (350 g) risotto rice

3 cups (750 ml) chicken stock, (home-made or bouillon cube), boiling

¼ cup (60 g) butter, cut into pieces

½ cup (60 g) freshly grated Parmesan

1 tablespoon finely chopped parsley

SERVES 4

PREPARATION 15 min

COOKING 30 min

DIFFICULTY level 2

Risotto
with zucchini flowers

Heat the oil in a large saucepan over medium heat. Add the shallots and sauté until transparent, 3–4 minutes. • Add the zucchini and one-third of the chopped zucchini flowers. Sauté until the flowers begin to soften, 2–3 minutes. • Add the rice and sauté for 2 minutes. • Pour in the wine and cook until it evaporates, 2–3 minutes. • Begin adding the stock, 1/2 cup (125 ml) at a time, cooking and stirring until each addition has been absorbed and the rice is tender, 15–18 minutes. • Add the remaining chopped zucchini flowers and the basil. Mix well and remove from the heat. • Stir in the Parmesan and butter. Season with salt and pepper. Cover and let rest for 2 minutes. • Garnish with the whole zucchini flowers and serve hot.

2 tablespoons extra-virgin olive oil
2 shallots, finely chopped
12 oz (350 g) small zucchini (courgettes), cut into small cubes
8 oz (250 g) zucchini flowers, coarsely chopped + 1–2 extra whole, to garnish
1³⁄₄ cups (350 g) risotto rice
1/3 cup (90 ml) dry white wine
3 cups (750 ml) vegetable stock, (homemade or bouillon cube), boiling
Leaves from 3 sprigs of basil, torn
1/2 cup (60 g) freshly grated Parmesan
1/4 cup (60 g) butter
Salt and freshly ground black pepper

SERVES 4
PREPARATION 10 min
COOKING 20 min
DIFFICULTY level 2

Oriental Risotto
with long-grain rice and peas

Mix together the cream, cloves, saffron, and cinnamon in a small bowl. Set aside. • Heat the oil in a large saucepan over low heat. Add the ginger and sauté for 2 minutes. • Add the rice and peas and sauté for 2 minutes more. • Add the water and season with salt. Mix well and bring to a boil. Simmer until the rice has absorbed all the liquid, about 10 minutes. Add a little more water during the cooking time if the rice begins to stick to the saucepan. • Remove the cinnamon from the cream and discard. • Stir the cream into the rice and mix well. Cover and cook over very low heat until the rice has absorbed the cream and is tender, about 5 minutes. • Transfer to a serving dish and serve hot.

⅔ cup (150 ml) heavy (double) cream
4 cloves, crushed
Pinch of saffron strands
1 cinnamon stick
¼ cup (60 ml) extra-virgin olive oil
½ oz (15 g) fresh ginger, peeled and thinly sliced
1½ cups (300 g) long-grain rice
1 cup (150 g) fresh or frozen peas
About 2⅓ cups (600 ml) water, boiling + a little more if required
Salt

SERVES 4

PREPARATION: 15 min

COOKING 45 min

DIFFICULTY level 2

Oriental Risotto

with chicken, beef, and shrimp

Heat half the oil in a large frying pan. Sauté the chicken until tender and cooked, 6–8 minutes. Set aside. • In the same pan, heat the remaining oil and sauté the leek and garlic until transparent, about 3 minutes. • Add the beef and season with salt and pepper. Sauté until the beef is lightly browned, 6–8 minutes. • Add the chicken mixture, rice, peas, and stock. Stir well, then cover and cook over low heat until the rice is tender, about 15 minutes. Add the shrimp 3 minutes before the rice is ready. • Add the eggs, stirring until they are cooked and firm. • Serve hot with the soy sauce passed separately.

⅓ cup (90 ml) extra-virgin olive oil

1 boneless, skinless chicken breast, cut in thin strips

1 leek, thinly sliced

2 cloves garlic, finely chopped

8 oz (250 g) beef, cut in thin strips

Salt and freshly ground black pepper

1¾ cups (350 g) long-grain rice

1 cup (150 g) frozen peas

3 cups (750 ml) chicken stock, (homemade or bouillon cube), boiling

10 oz (300 g) shrimp (prawn) tails, shelled and deveined

2 large eggs

Soy sauce, to serve

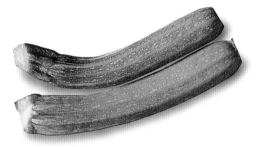

SERVES 4
PREPARATION 10 min
COOKING 25 min
DIFFICULTY level 2

Risotto
with apples and zucchini

Place the apples in a bowl. Drizzle with the lemon juice. • Heat the oil in a large frying pan over medium heat. Add the onion and sauté until transparent, 3–4 minutes. • Add the potatoes, zucchini, and carrot. Sauté for 2 minutes. • Add the rice and sauté for 2 minutes. • Add ½ cup (125 ml) of the stock and cook until it is absorbed. Add the apples and lemon juice and mix well. Keep adding the stock, ½ cup (125 ml) at a time, cooking and stirring until each addition has been absorbed and the rice is tender, 15–18 minutes. • Remove from the heat and stir in the soy sauce, curry powder, dill, and saffron. Season with salt and pepper and mix gently. • Remove from the heat, cover and let rest for 1 minute. Garnish with dill and serve hot.

2 green apples, cored and thinly sliced
Juice of 1 lemon
2 tablespoons extra-virgin olive oil
1 large onion, finely chopped
4 medium potatoes, peeled and cut into small cubes
3 medium zucchini (courgettes), cut into small cubes
1 large carrot, cut into small cubes
1¾ cups (350 g) risotto rice
3 cups (750 ml) vegetable stock, (homemade or bouillon cube), boiling
1 teaspoon dark soy sauce
1 teaspoon curry powder
2 tablespoons finely chopped dill + extra, to garnish
Pinch of saffron strands
Salt and freshly ground black pepper

SERVES 4
PREPARATION 15 min
COOKING 35 min
DIFFICULTY level 1

Risotto
with bell peppers

Heat the oil in a large frying pan over medium heat. Add the onion and garlic and sauté until the onion is transparent, 3–4 minutes. • Add the bell peppers and sauté until tender, 5–7 minutes. • Add the rice and sauté for 2 minutes. • Stir in the wine and cook until it evaporates, 2–3 minutes. • Begin adding the stock, 1/2 cup (125 ml) at a time, cooking and stirring until each addition has been absorbed and the rice is tender, 15–18 minutes. • Season with salt and mix well. Remove from the heat and stir in the basil, parsley, and cilantro. Cover and let rest for 1 minute. • Garnish with the basil and serve hot.

1/4 cup (60 ml) extra-virgin olive oil
1 large onion, finely chopped
1 clove garlic, finely chopped
2 large red bell peppers (capsicums), seeded and thinly sliced
2 large yellow bell peppers (capsicums), seeded and thinly sliced
1 3/4 cups (350 g) risotto rice
1/3 cup (90 ml) dry white wine
3 cups (750 ml) vegetable stock, (homemade or bouillon cube), boiling
Salt
1 tablespoon finely chopped basil + extra, to garnish
1 tablespoon finely chopped parsley
1 tablespoon finely chopped cilantro (coriander)

SERVES 4

PREPARATION 20 min

COOKING 55 min

DIFFICULTY level 2

Risotto
with pumpkin

Put the water, half the carrot, 1 onion, 1 stalk celery, and the fennel in a large saucepan over medium heat. Add the parsley and bring to a boil. • Cut two-thirds of the pumpkin into small cubes. Add to the saucepan. Simmer until the pumpkin is tender, 10–15 minutes. Chop the pumpkin and vegetables in a food processor to make a smooth purée. Filter the cooking liquid through a fine mesh strainer and set aside. • Slice the remaining pumpkin thinly. • Heat the oil in a large frying pan over medium heat. Add the pumpkin and sauté until tender, 7–8 minutes. Set aside. • Melt the butter in the same pan over medium heat. Add the finely chopped carrot, onion, celery, and rosemary and sauté until the vegetables are tender, about 5 minutes. • Add the rice and sauté for 2 minutes. • Stir in the Marsala and cook until it evaporates, 2–3 minutes. • Add the pumpkin purée and $\frac{1}{2}$ cup (125 ml) of the reserved cooking liquid. Keep adding the cooking liquid, $\frac{1}{2}$ cup (125 ml) at a time, cooking and stirring until each addition has been absorbed and the rice is tender, 15–18 minutes. • Add the cream, milk, lemon zest, and Parmesan. Season with salt and pepper. • Remove from the heat, cover, and let rest for 2 minutes. • Arrange the sautéed pumpkin on top and serve hot.

6 cups (1.5 liters) water
1 large carrot, $\frac{1}{2}$ finely chopped
2 small onions, 1 finely chopped
2 celery sticks, 1 finely chopped
$\frac{1}{2}$ fennel bulb, finely chopped
2 sprigs parsley
14 oz (400 g) fresh pumpkin flesh
3 tablespoons extra-virgin olive oil
2 tablespoons butter
1 tablespoon finely chopped rosemary
$1\frac{3}{4}$ cups (350 g) risotto rice
$\frac{1}{3}$ cup (90 ml) dry Marsala wine
$\frac{1}{3}$ cup (90 ml) heavy (double) cream
$\frac{1}{4}$ cup (60 ml) milk
Grated zest of 1 lemon
$\frac{1}{4}$ cup (30 g) freshly grated Parmesan
Salt and freshly ground black pepper

Risotto
with spinach and bacon

Cook the spinach in salted boiling water until tender, 3–4 minutes. Drain, squeeze out excess moisture, and chop finely. • Melt 4 tablespoons of butter in a large frying pan over medium heat. Add the onion and sauté until transparent, 3–4 minutes. • Add the rice and sauté for 2 minutes. • Add ½ cup (125 ml) of the stock and cook until it is absorbed. Add the spinach and mix well. Keep adding the stock, ½ cup (125 ml) at a time, cooking and stirring until each addition has been absorbed and the rice is tender, 15–18 minutes. • Cook the bacon in a small frying pan over medium heat until crisp, about 5 minutes. • Season the risotto with pepper and stir in the remaining butter and the Parmesan. Remove from the heat, cover, and let rest for 2 minutes • Spoon the risotto into serving dishes and top each portion with slices of bacon. Serve hot.

1 lb (500 g) fresh or frozen spinach
Salt
⅓ cup (90 g) butter
1 small onion, chopped finely
1¾ cups (350 g) risotto rice
3 cups (750 ml) vegetable stock, (homemade or bouillon cube), boiling
8–12 slices bacon
Freshly ground black pepper
½ cup (60 g) freshly grated Parmesan

SERVES 4
PREPARATION 15 min
COOKING 40 min
DIFFICULTY level 2

Risotto
with asparagus and peas

Combine the cream and saffron in a bowl and mix well. • Melt 2 tablespoons of the butter in a large frying pan over medium heat. Add the asparagus and two-thirds of the onion and sauté for 2 minutes. Season with salt and pepper. Add a ladle of the stock and cook until the asparagus is just tender, 6–7 minutes. • Add the peas and cook until all the vegetables are tender, 3–4 minutes. • Add the cream and mix well. Simmer for 1–2 minutes more then remove from the heat. • Melt 2 tablespoons of the butter in another large frying pan over medium heat. Add the remaining onion and sauté until transparent, 3–4 minutes. • Add the rice and sauté for 2 minutes. • Pour in the wine and cook until it evaporates, 2–3 minutes. • Begin adding the stock, $1/2$ cup (125 ml) at a time, cooking and stirring until each addition has been absorbed and the rice is tender, 15–18 minutes. • Season with salt. Remove from the heat and stir in the remaining butter and the Parmesan. Cover, and let rest for 1 minute. • Spoon the asparagus mixture over the risotto. Serve hot.

$1/3$ cup (60 ml) heavy (double) cream
Pinch of saffron strands
$1/3$ cup (90 g) butter
8 oz (250 g) asparagus tips, cut into short sections
3 small onions, finely chopped
Salt and freshly ground black pepper
3 cups (750 ml) vegetable stock, (homemade or bouillon cube), boiling
1 cup (150 g) frozen peas
$1^3/4$ cups (350 g) risotto rice
$1/3$ cup (90 ml) dry white wine
$1/2$ cup (60 g) freshly grated Parmesan

SERVES 4

PREPARATION 10 min

COOKING 40 min

DIFFICULTY level 1

Risotto
with potato and cabbage

Heat 3 tablespoons of oil in a small frying pan over medium heat. Add the potatoes and sauté until tender and golden brown, 8–10 minutes. Remove from the heat. • Heat the remaining oil in a large frying pan over medium heat. Add the rice and sauté for 2 minutes. • Pour in the wine and cook until it evaporates, 2–3 minutes. • Add the onion and cabbage and sauté for 3 minutes. • Begin adding the stock $1/2$ cup (125 ml) at a time, cooking and stirring until each addition has been absorbed and the rice is tender, 15–18 minutes. • Add the potatoes. Season with salt and mix well. • Garnish with parsley and serve hot.

$1/3$ cup (90 ml) extra-virgin olive oil
2 large potatoes, peeled and cut into small cubes
$1^3/4$ cups (350 g) risotto rice
$1/3$ cup (90 ml) dry white wine
1 large onion, chopped finely
8 oz (250 g) cabbage, shredded
3 cups (750 ml) vegetable stock, (homemade or bouillon cube), boiling
Salt
1 tablespoon finely chopped parsley, to garnish

SERVES 4

PREPARATION 15 min

COOKING 50 min

DIFFICULTY level 1

Risotto
with leeks and fontina

Heat the honey in a small saucepan over medium heat until it begins to caramelize, 3–4 minutes. • Add the wine and let it reduce over medium heat until the sauce is thick, about 15 minutes. Remove from the heat and cover. • Melt 4 tablespoons of butter in a large frying pan over medium heat. Add the leeks and sauté until they are transparent, 3–4 minutes. • Add the rice and sauté for 2 minutes. • Begin adding the stock, ½ cup (125 ml) at a time, cooking and stirring until each addition has been absorbed and the rice is tender, 15–18 minutes. • Season with salt and pepper and mix well. Remove from the heat. • Add the remaining butter and the Fontina. Drizzle with the honey and wine sauce and serve hot.

3 tablespoons honey

2 cups (500 ml) fruity red wine

⅓ cup (90 g) butter

4 small leeks, cleaned and finely sliced

1¾ cups (350 g) risotto rice

3 cups (750 ml) beef stock, (homemade or bouillon cube), boiling

Salt and freshly ground black pepper

3 oz (90 g) Fontina or other mild firm cheese, cut into small cubes

SERVES 4

PREPARATION 15 min

COOKING 35 min

DIFFICULTY level 1

Risotto
with beans and balsamic vinegar

Sauté the pancetta in a small frying pan over medium heat until crisp and lightly browned, 3–4 minutes. Remove from the heat. • Melt 2 tablespoons of the butter in a large frying pan over medium heat. Add the onions and sauté until transparent, 3–4 minutes. • Add the fava beans and $\frac{1}{2}$ cup (125 ml) of the stock. Season with salt, cover, and cook until the beans are tender, about 10 minutes. • Transfer one-third of the beans to a food processor and chop until smooth. • Add the rice to the frying pan and sauté for 2 minutes. • Pour in the wine and cook until it evaporates. • Begin adding the stock, $\frac{1}{2}$ cup (125 ml) at a time, cooking and stirring until each addition has been absorbed and the rice is tender, 15–18 minutes. • Stir in the bean purée, Parmesan, and remaining butter. • Sprinkle with the pancetta and Pecorino. Drizzle with balsamic vinegar and serve hot.

3 oz (90 g) pancetta or bacon, chopped
$\frac{1}{4}$ cup (60 g) butter
2 small onions, chopped finely
2 lb (1 kg) fresh or frozen fava (broad) beans
3 cups (750 ml) vegetable stock, (homemade or bouillon cube), boiling
Salt
$1\frac{3}{4}$ cups (350 g) risotto rice
$\frac{1}{3}$ cup (90 ml) dry white wine
$\frac{1}{2}$ cup (60 g) freshly grated Parmesan
2 oz (60 g) Pecorino cheese, cut into flakes
2 tablespoons balsamic vinegar

SERVES 4
PREPARATION 10 min
COOKING 25 min
DIFFICULTY level 1

Risotto

with champagne and cilantro

Melt 2 tablespoons of the butter in a large frying pan over medium heat. Add the onion and sauté until transparent, 3–4 minutes. • Add the rice and sauté for 2 minutes. • Pour in the champagne and cook until it evaporates, about 3 minutes. • Begin adding the stock, ¹/₂ cup (125 ml) at a time, cooking and stirring until each addition has been absorbed and the rice is tender, 15–18 minutes. • Season with salt and pepper. Remove from the heat. Stir in the remaining butter. Cover and let rest for 1 minute. • Sprinkle with cilantro and Parmesan. Serve hot.

¹/₄ cup (60 g) butter
1 large onion, finely chopped
1³/₄ cups (350 g) risotto rice
³/₄ cup (200 ml) champagne
3 cups (750 ml) chicken stock, (homemade or bouillon cube), boiling
Salt and freshly ground black pepper
2 tablespoons finely chopped cilantro (coriander)
3 oz (90 g) Parmesan, cut into flakes

Risotto
with sausage and sage

Heat the oil in a small frying pan over medium heat. Add the sage and fry until crisp, about 2 minutes. Transfer to paper towels using a slotted spoon. Let drain. • Melt half the butter in a large frying pan over medium heat. Add the onion and sauté until transparent, 3–4 minutes. • Add the sausage and sauté until brown, about 5 minutes. • Add the rice and sauté for 2 minutes. • Stir in the wine and cook until it evaporates, 2–3 minutes. • Begin adding the stock, ½ cup (125 ml) at a time, cooking and stirring until each addition has been absorbed and the rice is tender, 15–18 minutes. • Season with salt and pepper. Stir in the remaining butter. Cover and let rest for 1 minute. Garnish with the sage leaves and serve hot.

3 tablespoons extra-virgin olive oil
8–10 leaves fresh sage
3 tablespoons butter
1 large onion, finely chopped
14 oz (400 g) Italian pork sausages, skinned and cut into bite-size pieces
1¾ cups (350 g) risotto rice
⅓ cup (90 ml) full bodied red wine
3 cups (750 ml) beef stock, (homemade or bouillon cube), boiling
Salt and freshly ground black pepper

SERVES 4

PREPARATION 15 min

COOKING 35 min

DIFFICULTY level 1

Risotto

with herbs and quails' eggs

Put the quails' eggs in a small saucepan of cold water. Bring to a boil. Cook for 2 minutes from the moment the water reaches a boil. Drain and cool under cold running water. Shell the eggs and cut in half. • Heat the oil in a large frying pan over medium heat. Add the onion and celery. Sauté until the vegetables have softened, about 5 minutes. • Add the rice and sauté for 2 minutes. • Pour in the wine and cook until it evaporates, 2–3 minutes. • Add the zucchini and mix well. • Begin adding the stock, ½ cup (125 ml) at a time, cooking and stirring until each addition has been absorbed and the rice is tender, 15–18 minutes. • Season with salt and pepper. Remove from the heat. Add the Parmesan, chervil, parsley, tarragon, chives, and basil. Mix well and top with the quails' eggs. Serve hot.

8 quails' eggs
¼ cup (60 ml) extra-virgin olive oil
1 large onion, finely chopped
2 stalks celery, finely chopped
1¾ cups (350 g) risotto rice
⅓ cup (90 ml) dry white wine
3 medium zucchini (courgettes), cut into 1-inch (3-cm) batons
3 cups (750 ml) vegetable stock, (homemade or bouillon cube), boiling
Salt and freshly ground black pepper
4 oz (125 g) Parmesan, cut in small cubes
Leaves from 3 sprigs of chervil
1 tablespoon finely chopped parsley
1 tablespoon finely chopped tarragon
1 tablespoon finely chopped chives
½ tablespoon finely chopped basil

SERVES 4

PREPARATION 15 min

COOKING 1 h

DIFFICULTY level 2

Risotto
with pears and goat cheese

Preheat the oven to 350°F (180°C/gas 4). • Cut one of the pears in quarters and remove the core. Slice very thinly and place the slices on a baking sheet lined with baking parchment. Bake, turning from time to time, until the slices have dried out, 15–20 minutes. Set aside. • Core and chop the remaining pears. • Place the wine in a small saucepan and bring to a boil over low heat. Simmer for 10 minutes. • Melt the butter in a large frying pan over medium heat. Add the shallot and sauté until transparent, 3–4 minutes. • Add the rice and sauté for 2 minutes. • Pour in the hot wine and cook until it evaporates, 2–3 minutes. • Add ½ cup (125 ml) of the stock and cook until it is absorbed. Add the chopped pears and mix well. Keep adding the stock, ½ cup (125 ml) at a time, cooking and stirring until each addition has been absorbed and the rice is tender, 15–18 minutes. • Season with salt and pepper. Remove from the heat. • Stir in the goat cheese and ginger. Cover and let rest for 2 minutes. • Top with the baked pears. Garnish with marjoram and serve hot.

3 large ripe pears
½ cup (125 ml) dry white wine
2 tablespoons butter
1 shallot, finely chopped
1¾ cups (350 g) risotto rice
3 cups (750 ml) vegetable stock, (homemade or bouillon cube), boiling
Salt and freshly ground black pepper
8 oz (250 g) fresh creamy goat cheese
2 tablespoons chopped candied ginger
Fresh marjoram, to garnish

Risotto

with peas and cheese

Bring the stock to a boil in a large saucepan over medium heat. Add half the peas and simmer until tender, 6–7 minutes. • Transfer to a food processor and chop until smooth. Return the mixture to the saucepan and keep warm. • Heat the oil in a large frying pan over medium heat. Add the pancetta and sauté until golden brown, 3–4 minutes. • Add the onion and sauté until transparent, 3–4 minutes. • Add the remaining peas and the rice and sauté for 2 minutes. • Begin adding the stock and pea mixture, $1/2$ cup (125 ml) at a time, cooking and stirring until each addition has been absorbed and the rice is tender, 15–18 minutes. • Season with salt. Remove from the heat. • Stir in the grated Parmesan. Cover and let rest for 2 minutes. • Sprinkle with the flakes of Parmesan and serve hot.

3 cups (750 ml) vegetable stock, (homemade or bouillon cube)

1 lb (500 g) fresh or frozen peas

$1/4$ cup (60 ml) extra-virgin olive oil

5 oz (150 g) pancetta or bacon, chopped

1 large onion, finely chopped

$1^3/_4$ cups (350 g) risotto rice

Salt

$1/2$ cup (60 g) freshly grated Parmesan

1 oz (30 g) Parmesan, cut into flakes

SERVES 4

PREPARATION 5 min + time to soak

COOKING 1 h 20 min

DIFFICULTY level 2

Risotto

with sausage and black-eyed peas

Cook the black-eyed peas with the bay leaf in a large pot of boiling water until tender, 40–50 minutes. Season with salt. Drain well and discard the bay leaf. • Melt 1 tablespoon of the butter in a small frying pan over medium heat. Add the rosemary and sausages and sauté until the sausages are lightly browned, 3–4 minutes. • Melt the remaining butter in a large frying pan over medium heat. Add the shallots and sauté until transparent, 3–4 minutes. • Add the rice and sauté for 2 minutes. • Pour in the wine and cook until it evaporates, 2–3 minutes. • Lower the heat and add the black-eyed peas. Begin adding the stock, $1/2$ cup (125 ml) at a time, cooking and stirring until each addition has been absorbed and the rice is tender, 15–18 minutes. • Season with salt and pepper. Remove from the heat. • Top with the sautéed sausage and serve hot.

5 oz (150 g) dried black-eyed peas, soaked overnight and drained
1 bay leaf
Salt
$1/4$ cup (60 g) butter
$1/2$ tablespoon finely chopped rosemary
12 oz (350 g) Italian sausages, skinned and cut into small cubes
2 shallots, finely chopped
$1^{3}/_{4}$ cups (350 g) risotto rice
$1/3$ cup (90 ml) dry white wine
3 cups (750 ml) vegetable stock, (homemade or bouillon cube), boiling
Freshly ground black pepper

Risotto
with prosciutto and fennel

Blanch the fennel leaves in boiling water for 2 minutes. Drain well and chop finely. • Heat the wine in a small saucepan over medium heat. • Heat the oil in a small frying pan over medium heat. Add half the prosciutto and sauté until crisp and lightly browned, 2–3 minutes. Drain on paper towels. • Melt half the butter in a large frying pan over medium heat. Add the onion and remaining prosciutto. Sauté until transparent, 3–4 minutes. • Add the rice and sauté for 2 minutes. • Pour in the hot wine and cook until it evaporates, 2–3 minutes. • Begin adding the stock, 1/2 cup (125 ml) at a time, cooking and stirring until each addition has been absorbed and the rice is tender, 15–18 minutes. • Season with salt and pepper. Remove from the heat. Stir in the remaining butter, the fennel, and Parmesan. Cover and let rest for 1 minute. • Sprinkle with the sautéed prosciutto and serve hot.

2 oz (60 g) fennel leaves
1/3 cup (90 ml) dry white wine
1/4 cup (60 ml) extra-virgin olive oil
5 oz (150 g) prosciutto (Parma ham), sliced into ribbons
1/4 cup (60 g) butter
1 large onion, finely chopped
13/4 cups (350 g) risotto rice
3 cups (750 ml) meat stock, (homemade or bouillon cube), boiling
Salt and freshly ground black pepper
1/2 cup (60 g) freshly grated Parmesan

SERVES 4

PREPARATION 45 min + I h to soak

COOKING I h

DIFFICULTY level 3

Pepper Risotto
with seafood sauce

Place the mussels and clams in a large pan over high heat. Cook until opened, 7–10 minutes. Discard any that do not open. Drain, reserving the cooking juices. • Filter the juices through a strainer and set aside. • Remove the shells from the clams and half of the mussels. • Preheat the broiler (grill). Grill the bell peppers, turning often, until charred all over, 8–10 minutes. Place in a plastic bag. Seal the bag and let rest for 2–3 minutes. Remove from the bag. Remove the skins and seeds and slice thinly. • Heat half the oil in a large frying pan over medium heat. Add the onion and sauté until transparent, 3–4 minutes. • Stir in the bell peppers. • Add the rice and sauté for 2 minutes. • Pour in 6 tablespoons of the wine and cook until it evaporates, 2–3 minutes. • Lower the heat and begin adding the stock, 1/2 cup (125 ml) at a time, cooking and stirring until each addition has been absorbed and the rice is tender, 15–18 minutes. • Season with salt and pepper. Remove from the heat. Cover and let rest for 2 minutes. • Heat the remaining oil in a large frying pan over medium heat. Add the garlic and sauté until pale gold. Discard the garlic. Stir in the reserved cooking juices. Add the remaining wine and let reduce for 2–3 minutes. • Add the mussels and clams. Sauté for 2 minutes. Season with salt and pepper. Add the parsley, basil, and marjoram. • Spoon the seafood sauce over the risotto and serve hot.

- I lb (500 g) mussels, in shell, soaked in cold water for I hour and scrubbed
- I lb (500 g) clams, in shell, soaked in cold water for I hour
- 2 large red bell peppers (capsicums)
- 1/3 cup (90 ml) extra-virgin olive oil
- I large onion, finely chopped
- 1 3/4 cups (350 g) risotto rice
- 1/2 cup (125 ml) dry white wine
- 3 cups (750 ml) vegetable stock, (homemade or bouillon cube), boiling
- Salt and freshly ground black pepper
- I clove garlic, lightly crushed but whole
- I tablespoon finely chopped parsley
- 1/2 tablespoon finely chopped basil
- 1/2 tablespoon finely chopped marjoram

SERVES 4–6

PREPARATION 35 min + overnight chilling

COOKING 1 h 25 min

DIFFICULTY level 3

Risotto
with cod and orange

Fillet the cod, reserving the bones. • Chop the flesh finely and transfer to a large bowl. • Remove the zest from the oranges using a sharp knife and cut into julienne strips. • Peel the oranges and chop the flesh. • Heat 2 tablespoons of the oil in a large frying pan over medium heat. Add one onion, the carrot, and leek and sauté until softened, 5 minutes. Add the tomatoes, thyme, 1 bay leaf, and the orange flesh. Stir this mixture into the prepared cod. Add the chile pepper and mix well. Cover and chill overnight. • Put the reserved cod bones into a large pot. Add the water, 1/2 cup (125 ml) of wine, and the remaining bay leaf. Season with salt and pepper. Bring to a boil, then simmer for 45 minutes. Remove from the heat and let cool. Filter the stock. • Put the cod and its marinade in a food processor. Discard the bay leaf. Chop until smooth. • Heat the remaining oil in a large frying pan over medium heat. Add the remaining onion and sauté until transparent, 3–4 minutes. • Add the rice and sauté for 2 minutes. • Pour in the remaining wine and cook until it evaporates, 2–3 minutes. Begin adding the stock, 1/2 cup (125 ml) at a time, cooking and stirring until each addition has been absorbed and the rice is tender, 15–18 minutes. Stir in the cod mixture and the orange zest. • Serve hot.

2 lb (1 kg) fresh cod
2 large ripe oranges
1/4 cup (60 ml) extra-virgin olive oil
2 small onions, finely chopped
1 medium carrot, peeled and finely chopped
1 small leek, thinly sliced
1/2 cup (125 g) canned tomatoes, with juice
1 tablespoon finely chopped thyme
2 bay leaves
Pinch of ground chile pepper
6 cups (1.5 liters) water
3/4 cup (200 ml) dry white wine
Salt and freshly ground black pepper
2 cups (400 g) risotto rice

Risotto
with seafood

Heat 3 tablespoons of oil with the garlic in a large saucepan over high heat. Add the mussels and clams and cook until they open, 7–10 minutes. Drain, reserving the cooking juices. Remove most of the shells. • Heat 3 tablespoons of the remaining oil in a large frying pan over medium heat. Add the onion, carrot, and celery. Sauté until transparent, 3–4 minutes. Add the squid and sauté for 2 minutes. • Pour in the wine and cook until it evaporates, 2–3 minutes. • Add the rice and sauté for 2 minutes. Add the reserved cooking juices and cook until absorbed. • Begin adding the stock, $\frac{1}{2}$ cup (125 ml) at a time, cooking and stirring until each addition has been absorbed and the rice is tender, 15–18 minutes. Season with salt and pepper. • Heat the remaining oil in a large frying pan over high heat. Add the shrimps. Sauté for 2 minutes. Add the clams and mussels. • Stir into the risotto. Cook for 2 minutes. Remove from the heat. Cover and let rest for 2 minutes. Sprinkle with parsley and serve hot.

$\frac{1}{2}$ cup (125 ml) extra-virgin olive oil

1 clove garlic, lightly crushed but whole

14 oz (400 g) mussels, in shell, soaked in cold water for 1 hour and scrubbed

14 oz (400 g) fresh clams, in shell, soaked in cold water for 1 hour

1 small onion, finely chopped

1 small carrot, finely chopped

1 stalk celery, finely chopped

8 oz (250 g) baby squid, cleaned and sliced

$\frac{3}{4}$ cup (125 ml) dry white wine

$1\frac{3}{4}$ cups (350 g) risotto rice

3 cups (750 ml) fish stock, (homemade or bouillon cube), boiling

Salt and freshly ground black pepper

5 oz (150 g) shelled shrimps (prawns)

8 large shrimp (tiger prawns)

1 tablespoon finely chopped parsley

SERVES 4

PREPARATION 15 min

COOKING 1 h 15 min

DIFFICULTY level 2

Risotto
with chicken wings

Melt 2 tablespoons of butter in a saucepan over medium-high heat. Add half the shallots, sage, and chicken and season with salt. Sauté until the chicken is sealed all over, 3–4 minutes. • Cover and cook over low heat for 15 minutes. • Add ⅓ cup (90 ml) of the wine. Cover and cook until the chicken is very tender, about 25 minutes more. • Heat the oil in a large frying pan over medium heat. Add the remaining shallots and sauté until transparent, about 3 minutes. Add the rice and sauté for 2 minutes. • Pour in the remaining wine and cook until it evaporates, 2–3 minutes. • Begin adding the stock, ½ cup (125 ml) at a time, cooking and stirring until each addition has been absorbed and the rice is tender, 15–18 minutes. • Season with salt and pepper. Stir in the remaining butter, the Parmesan, and ground cinnamon. Arrange the chicken on top. Sprinkle with the orange zest and parsley. • Garnish with the cinnamon stick and serve hot.

¼ cup (60 g) butter
4 shallots, sliced
4 sage leaves, torn
8 chicken wings
Salt
⅔ cup (150 ml) dry white wine
¼ cup (60 g) extra-virgin olive oil
1¾ cups (350 g) risotto rice
3 cups (750 ml) chicken stock, (homemade or bouillon cube), boiling
Freshly ground black pepper
½ cup (60 g) freshly grated Parmesan
½ teaspoon ground cinnamon
Zest of 1 orange, cut into julienne strips
1 tablespoon finely chopped parsley
1 cinnamon stick, to garnish

47

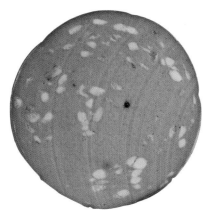

SERVES 4
PREPARATION 15 min
COOKING 30 min
DIFFICULTY level 2

Risotto
with mortadella and artichokes

Remove the tough outer leaves from the artichokes. Cut off the top third of the leaves. Cut in half and scrape out any fuzzy inner core, Slice finely. • Heat the oil in a large frying pan over medium heat. Add the shallot and artichokes and sauté until the shallot is transparent, 3–4 minutes. • Add the rice and sauté for 2 minutes. • Pour in the wine and cook until it evaporates, 2–3 minutes. • Begin adding the stock, 1/2 cup (125 ml) at a time, cooking and stirring until each addition has been absorbed and the rice is tender, 15–18 minutes. • Season with salt and pepper. • Stir in the mortadella. Remove from the heat. • Add the butter and Parmesan. Mix well, cover, and let rest for 2 minutes. • Sprinkle with the parsley and serve hot.

4 artichokes
2 tablespoons extra-virgin olive oil
1 shallot, finely chopped
1¾ cups (350 g) risotto rice
1/3 cup (90 ml) dry white wine
3 cups (750 ml) vegetable stock,
   (homemade or bouillon cube),
   boiling
Salt and freshly ground black pepper
5 oz (150 g) mortadella,
   cut into small cubes
1/4 cup (60 g) butter
3/4 cup (90 g) freshly grated Parmesan
1 tablespoon finely chopped parsley

SERVES 4
PREPARATION 10 min
COOKING 30 min
DIFFICULTY level 1

Risotto
with pancetta and peas

Heat 2 tablespoons of the butter in a large frying pan over medium heat. Add the onion and pancetta and sauté until the onion is transparent and the pancetta lightly browned, about 5 minutes. • Add the peas, 2 tablespoons of the parsley, and ½ cup (125 ml) of the stock. Cover and cook until the peas are tender, about 10 minutes. • Stir in the rice and then begin adding the stock, ½ cup (125 ml) at a time, cooking and stirring until each addition has been absorbed and the rice is tender, 15–18 minutes. • Season with salt and pepper. Remove from the heat. Stir in the remaining butter and the Parmesan. Cover and let rest for 2 minutes. • Sprinkle with the remaining parsley and serve hot.

¼ cup (60 g) butter
1 large white onion, finely chopped
2 oz (60 g) pancetta, chopped
2 lb (1 kg) fresh or frozen peas
3 tablespoons finely chopped parsley
4 cups (1 liter) vegetable stock, (homemade or bouillon cube), boiling
1¾ cups (350 g) risotto rice
Salt and freshly ground black pepper
⅓ cup (30 g) freshly grated Parmesan

SERVES 4

PREPARATION 15 min

COOKING 30 min

DIFFICULTY level 1

Risotto
with mushrooms and thyme

Melt 1 tablespoon of the butter with the oil in a large saucepan over medium heat. Add the onion and garlic and sauté until the onion is transparent, 3–4 minutes. • Add the mushrooms and sauté until they begin to soften, 3–4 minutes. • Add the rice and sauté for 2 minutes. • Pour in the wine and cook until it evaporates, 2–3 minutes. • Begin adding the stock, ½ cup (125 ml) at a time, cooking and stirring until each addition has been absorbed and the rice is tender, 15–18 minutes. • Stir in the remaining butter and the Parmesan. Season with salt and pepper. • Add the thyme and mix well. Remove from the heat and let rest for 1 minute. • Serve hot.

2 tablespoons butter
2 tablespoons extra-virgin olive oil
1 small onion, finely sliced
1 clove garlic, finely chopped
12 oz (350 g) button mushrooms, sliced
1¾ cups (350 g) risotto rice
⅓ cup (90 ml) dry white wine
3 cups (750 ml) vegetable stock, (homemade or bouillon cube), boiling
½ cup (60 g) freshly grated Parmesan
Salt and freshly ground black pepper
2 tablespoons finely chopped thyme

SERVES 4

PREPARATION 15 min

COOKING 55 min

DIFFICULTY level 2

Risotto
with leeks, lemon, and rosemary

Melt 4 tablespoons of the butter in a large frying pan over low heat. Add the leeks and sauté until they begin to soften, 2–3 minutes. • Add the water and season with salt. Cook until the leeks begin to break down, about 20 minutes. • Heat the oil in another large frying pan over medium heat. Add the shallot and sauté until transparent, 3–4 minutes. • Add the rice and sauté for 2 minutes. • Pour in the wine and cook until it evaporates, 2–3 minutes. • Add the leeks and their cooking juices, and mix well. • Add $\frac{1}{2}$ cup (125 ml) of the stock and cook until it is absorbed. Stir in the lemon zest and rosemary and season with salt and pepper. Keep adding the stock, $\frac{1}{2}$ cup (125 ml) at a time, cooking and stirring until each addition has been absorbed and the rice is tender, 15–18 minutes. • Stir in the remaining butter and the Parmesan. • Garnish with the lemon zest and rosemary and serve hot.

$\frac{1}{3}$ cup (90 g) butter
2 small leeks, finely sliced
$\frac{1}{3}$ cup (90 ml) water
Salt
2 tablespoons extra-virgin olive oil
1 shallot, finely chopped
$1\frac{3}{4}$ cups (350 g) risotto rice
$\frac{1}{3}$ cup (90 ml) dry white wine
3 cups (750 ml) vegetable stock, (homemade or bouillon cube), boiling
Freshly grated zest of 1 lemon
2 tablespoons finely chopped rosemary
Freshly ground black pepper
$\frac{2}{3}$ cup (100 g) freshly grated Parmesan
Zest of 1 lemon, cut into julienne strips, to garnish
Sprigs of rosemary, to garnish

Risotto
with leeks and parmesan

Melt 4 tablespoons of the butter in a large frying pan over medium heat. Add the leeks and sauté until tender, about 5 minutes. • Add the rice and sauté for 2 minutes. • Pour in the wine and cook until it evaporates, 2–3 minutes. • Begin adding the stock, ½ cup (125 ml) at a time, cooking and stirring until each addition has been absorbed and the rice is tender, 15–18 minutes. • Stir in the remaining butter and the Parmesan. Season with salt and pepper. Remove from the heat and let rest for 1 minute. • Serve hot.

⅓ cup (90 g) butter
3 small leeks, finely sliced
1¾ cups (350 g) risotto rice
⅓ cup (90 ml) dry white wine
3 cups (750 ml) vegetable stock, (homemade or bouillon cube), boiling
⅔ cup (100 g) freshly grated Parmesan
Salt and freshly ground black pepper

SERVES 4

PREPARATION 10 min

COOKING 45 min

DIFFICULTY level 1

Risotto

with chicken and marsala

Bring the Marsala wine to a boil in a small saucepan over low heat. Simmer until reduced to half its original volume, 10–15 minutes. Remove from the heat. • Heat the oil in a large frying pan over medium heat. Add the onion and sauté until transparent, 3–4 minutes. • Add the chicken and sauté until lightly browned all over, 4–5 minutes. • Add the rice and sauté for 2 minutes. • Begin adding the stock, ½ cup (125 ml) at a time, cooking and stirring until each addition has been absorbed and the rice is tender, 15–18 minutes. • Add the haricot beans and season with salt and pepper. Mix well and remove from the heat. Let rest for 1 minute. • Drizzle with the reduced Marsala and serve hot.

1 cup (250 ml) dry Marsala wine
2 tablespoons extra-virgin olive oil
1 medium onion, finely chopped
1 boneless, skinless chicken breast, cut into bite-size chunks
1¾ cups (350 g) risotto rice
3 cups (750 ml) vegetable stock, (homemade or bouillon cube), boiling
Salt and freshly ground black pepper
1 cup (250 g) canned haricot beans, drained

SERVES 4

PREPARATION 10 min

COOKING 30 min

DIFFICULTY level 2

Risotto
with shrimps and orange

Cook the shrimps in a steamer until tender, 3–5 minutes. Set aside in a warm oven. • Melt 4 tablespoons of the butter in a large frying pan over medium heat. Add the onion and sauté until transparent, 3–4 minutes. • Add the rice and sauté for 2 minutes. • Pour in the wine and cook until it evaporates, 2–3 minutes. • Add ½ cup (125 ml) of the stock and cook until it is absorbed. Stir in the orange zest. • Keep adding the stock, ½ cup (125 ml) at a time, cooking and stirring until each addition has been absorbed and the rice is tender, 15–18 minutes. • Add the remaining butter and half the Parmesan. Season with salt and pepper. • Beat together the egg yolks and milk in a small bowl. Add this mixture to the risotto and mix well. Cook for 2 minutes, stirring constantly. • Stir in the remaining Parmesan. Remove from the heat and let rest for 1 minute. • Arrange the steamed shrimps on top and serve hot.

36 large fresh shrimps (prawns)
⅓ cup (90 g) butter
1 small onion, finely chopped
1¾ cups (350 g) risotto rice
⅓ cup (90 ml) dry white wine
3 cups (750 ml) vegetable stock, (homemade or bouillon cube), boiling
Freshly grated zest of 1 orange
1 cup (125 g) freshly grated Parmesan
Salt and freshly ground black pepper
2 large egg yolks
½ cup (125 ml) milk

SERVES 4

PREPARATION 10 min

COOKING 25 min

DIFFICULTY level 1

Risotto
with ham and zucchini

Melt the butter in a large frying pan over medium heat. Add the shallot and sauté until transparent, 3–4 minutes. • Add the rice and sauté for 2 minutes. • Stir in the wine and cook until it evaporates, 2–3 minutes. • Add ½ cup (125 ml) of the stock and cook until it is absorbed. Stir in the zucchini and season with salt and pepper. Keep adding the stock, ½ cup (125 ml) at a time, cooking and stirring until each addition has been absorbed and the rice is tender, 15–18 minutes. • Add the ham and mix well. Stir in the Parmesan and parsley. Serve hot.

¼ cup (60 g) butter
1 shallot, finely chopped
1¾ cups (350 g) risotto rice
⅓ cup (90 ml) dry white wine
3 cups (750 ml) vegetable stock, (homemade or bouillon cube), boiling
12 oz (350 g) zucchini (courgettes), thinly sliced
Salt and freshly ground black pepper
4 oz (125 g) ham, chopped
½ cup (60 g) freshly grated Parmesan
2 tablespoons finely chopped parsley

Risotto
with pumpkin and mushrooms

Bring the stock to a boil in a large saucepan over medium heat. Add the pumpkin, a sprig of rosemary, and the garlic. Simmer until the pumpkin is tender, 10–15 minutes. Discard the garlic and rosemary. • Transfer the pumpkin to a bowl using a slotted spoon. Keep the stock hot. • Heat 3 tablespoons of the oil in a small frying pan with the remaining rosemary and the orange zest. Sauté for 2 minutes then remove from the heat. Discard the rosemary. Set aside. • Heat the remaining oil in a large frying pan over medium heat. Add the onion and sauté until transparent, 3–4 minutes. • Add the mushrooms and sauté for 1–2 minutes. Season with salt and pepper • Add the rice and sauté for 2 minutes. • Add ½ cup (125 ml) of the stock and cook until it is absorbed. Stir in the pumpkin and season with salt and pepper. Keep adding the stock, ½ cup (125 ml) at a time, cooking and stirring until each addition has been absorbed and the rice is tender, 15–18 minutes. • Remove from the heat and stir in the orange zest and oil. • Cover and let rest for 1 minute. • Serve hot.

3 cups (750 ml) vegetable stock, (homemade or bouillon cube),

14 oz (400 g) fresh pumpkin flesh, cut into small cubes

2 sprigs of rosemary

1 clove garlic, lightly crushed but whole

⅓ cup (90 ml) extra-virgin olive oil

Zest of 1 orange, cut into julienne strips

1 large onion, finely chopped

8 oz (250 g) porcini (or other) mushrooms, sliced

Salt and freshly ground black pepper

1¾ cups (350 g) risotto rice

SERVES 4

PREPARATION 10 min

COOKING 25 min

DIFFICULTY level 1

Risotto

with smoked salmon

Warm 1 tablespoon of the oil in a small frying pan over medium-low heat. Add the salmon and sauté for 1 minute. Add the cream and mix gently. Remove from the heat and set aside. • Heat the remaining oil in a large frying pan over medium heat. Add the scallions and sauté until they begin to soften, 2 minutes. • Add the rice and sauté for 2 minutes. • Pour in wine and cook until it evaporates. • Begin adding the stock, 1/2 cup (125 ml) at a time, cooking and stirring until each addition has been absorbed and the rice is tender, 15–18 minutes. • Season with salt and pepper. • Add the salmon and cream and mix well. Remove from the heat and let rest for 1 minute. • Garnish with the parsley and serve hot.

3 tablespoons extra-virgin olive oil
4 oz (125 g) smoked salmon, cut into in very small pieces
1 cup (250 ml) heavy (double) cream
2 scallions (spring onions), chopped
1¾ cups (350 g) risotto rice
1/3 cup (90 ml) dry white wine
3 cups (750 ml) vegetable stock, (homemade or bouillon cube), boiling
Salt and freshly ground black pepper
1–2 tablespoons finely chopped parsley, to garnish

Index

Copyright © 2007 by McRae Books Srl

This English edition first published in 2007

Risotto

was created and produced by McRae Books Srl

Borgo Santa Croce, 8 – Florence (Italy)

info@mcraebooks.com

Publishers: Anne McRae and Marco Nardi

Project Director: Anne McRae

Design: Sara Mathews

Text: Carla Bardi

Editing: Osla Fraser

Photography: Mauro Corsi, Leonardo Pasquinelli, Gianni Petronio, Lorenzo Borri, Stefano Pratesi

Home Economist: Benedetto Rillo

Artbuying: McRae Books

Layouts: Adina Stefania Dragomir

Repro: Fotolito Raf, Florence

ISBN 978-88-89272-82-4

Printed and bound in China